WATER IN THE WEST:

THE SCARY TRUTH ABOUT
OUR MOST PRECIOUS RESOURCE

An Environmental Essay

By Lucinda Sue Crosby

Topics:

Lucinda Sue Crosby is an award winning journalist and environmentalist who spent five years as coordinator of education and conservation for a retail California water agency. The opinions expressed in this essay are the author's and not necessarily those of the sources sited, nor did the author receive compensation or remuneration from any of the sources consulted for the publication of this article.

No part of this essay may be reproduced in any form without the permission of its publisher.

Printed in the USA
LuckyCinda Publishing
www.luckycinda.com

"Sometimes, the proper perspective can only be gleaned from the big picture."

Lucinda Sue Crosby

WATER in the WEST

THE SCARY TRUTH ABOUT OUR MOST PRECIOUS RESOURCE

AN ENVIRONMENTAL ESSAY

The struggle to identify, develop and secure water sources is not new. In fact, archaeological and historical information tells us that the first conflicts in which the vital resource was in some way involved arose in the birthplaces of civilization.

But the undisputable evidence of international present-day water challenges has forced us all to begin taking a closer look at the state of H2O on Planet Earth.

- In 2007, U.S. Department of Agriculture scientist Robert Evans stated flatly, "Water will be the natural resource issue for the 21st century. It won't be oil; it will be water."

- At a United Nations summit in 2008, Dow Chemical Chairman and CEO Andrew Liveris underscored this sentiment when he said, "Water is today's issue. It is the oil of this century, not a question."

Globally, more than a billion people have no regular access to uncontaminated drinking water. Currently, cities in Brazil, Yemen and China are in the throes of water crises unseen in modern times. But in order to put this unwieldy and complex subject matter in a more digestible format, I'll start examining the topic of water woes where I live, in California.

During his last year in office, California Gov. Arnold Schwarzenegger declared a drought emergency in the Golden State. A subsequent off-the-charts snow pack year eased some of the strain on the state's water supply worries but California is still facing significant problems.

To whit: On January 17, 2014, Gov. Jerry Brown declared another drought emergency and the following spring, 29 retail and wholesale agencies accustomed to receiving supplements from state reservoirs had to look elsewhere. This decision affected 25 million California residents and a million agricultural acres and is the first such curtailment of water allotments since the inception of the State Water Project in 1954. By June, 17 small water districts spread across eight of the state's more arid counties were expected to actually run out of H2O. Through the fall and early winter, several man-made reservoirs were at historically low levels even after two large storms.

But this unprecedented dry spell with its attendant consequences only represents a portion of the Big Picture regarding California's growing water woes. Water infrastructure in many regions has long since fallen into disrepair, opening the floodgates for leaks, collapses and systemic contamination. For another, the fabled Delta's water supply, which provides over 60 per cent of California residents and millions of farm acres with precious liquid gold, faces numerous challenges: protective levees that are becoming more untrustworthy with every storm; salt water incursion to an already fragile eco system; and about a 40 percent loss of its fresh water which is diverted to other parts of the state.

Of course, California isn't the only state with H2O trouble. On the most basic level, a visit to any reputable U.S. drought map (http://droughtmonitor.unl.edu/) illustrates a harrowing tale. No wonder water utilities throughout the west and southwest and even in the mid-west and parts east are planning for what many experts are calling "foreseeable water shortages" over the next 20 to 30 years. Population trends are pointing to a gradual and growing shift of people to rural and desert areas. Coupled with contamination and climate change ... water agencies in the United States are beginning to feel unprecedented stress on their ability to provide constituents with clean, safe water.

The consensus of the world's hydrologists believe there is plenty of water on planet Earth – but much of it will have to be moved great distances and/or treated for arsenic, high mineral/salt content or even toxic chemicals to meet governmental drinking water standards. Simply put, the price of water is going up.

Renowned research groups, like the National Oceanic and Atmospheric Administration (NOAA) and the Stanford University Economics Department have been using the term "water crisis" for years. In 2008, the EPA predicted that 36 states would face a water crisis in the ensuing decade, give or take, and that's assuming normal rainfall patterns. Under extended drought, the number jumps to 46. On top of this, the EPA also estimates that about 40 percent of our lakes and rivers are not clean enough to drink.

Here are some specific eye-openers, taken from our nation's west and southwest where our most arid regions are located, that will only worsen without timely and substantial intervention:

THE PERILS OF OVER PUMPING

Item: According to a 10-year study conducted by the US Geological Survey, areas in the Coachella Valley floor sunk a total of 12 inches between 1995 and 2005. This was due to an attendant consequence called "subsidence," defined as a settling of the ground that occurs whenever groundwater is pumped out of natural underground storage at a faster rate than it can be replenished by precipitation. Continuous subsidence can pose a real threat to infrastructure like roadways, bridges and house foundations according to engineering experts.

It's not as if this problem manifested suddenly or recently. Coachella Valley water purveyors have been importing Colorado River water since 1948 and receive water from other expensive sources outside valley boundaries. Even so, the steadily increasing rate of overdraft and the accompanying and unavoidable subsidence proves that the mere act of importing more water doesn't solve all water woes.

These days, CV water users are looking at a host of future water quality problems that will surely manifest as water levels continue to drop: higher levels of naturally occurring dissolved minerals (like calcium and magnesium) that will eventually require treatment before meeting state and federal drinking water standards; the deepening of existing wells to reach a lower water table; and the construction of new wells. These mitigating practices come with heavy price tags and would add tens of millions of dollars to any water district's capital improvement budget.

One other hitch: Chromium 6 has been found to be in the valley's groundwater. Treating the water to federal standards is expected to cost each hook up an additional $500 annually.

Item: Back in the 1950s, over pumping of water in the San Joaquin Valley was estimated at up to 500,000 acre feet per year, with an acre foot (AF) equaling about 326,000 gallons. (http://pubs.usgs.gov/circ/circ1182/pdf/06SanJoaquinValley.pdf)

This means that 163 TRILLION more gallons of water were being taken out of the water cycle there each year than were being put back in. These days, groundwater levels in that region are dropping faster than ever before, averaging almost ten feet every 12 months.

As in the Coachella Valley, this chain of events promises ever more serious consequences. Over the past five or so decades, mostly rural parts of the San Joaquin Valley floor have sunk over 30 feet due to the region's continuous, decades-long "water mining." Population expansion in the area has led to more infrastructure and if/when those roads and house foundations become imperiled, the cost of their repair will be staggering.

The Good News: For the first time, Fresno and Sacramento are installing water meters to encourage water conservation. In the past, most residential water customers in those cities simply paid a so-called "flat rate," meaning that residents with wasteful habits had no incentive to conserve. Why would anyone bother to adopt water thrifty habits when their neighbors were paying the same monthly fee no matter how much water they wasted?

The Bad News: City of Sacramento Department of Utilities meter installation won't be completed until the state deadline for all homes and businesses – 2025. Fresno's Department of Public Utilities is faring a bit better – and finished its installation program in December of 2012. Throughout 2013-14, water utility workers will phase out flat rate billing in favor of bills generated by actual consumption. It remains to be seen if a substantial drop in per capita use is the end product of this effort but historical data collected from around the world predicts considerable water savings. **But is this conservation activity coming too late?** In 2014, the reservoirs of 12 small, rural towns in the San Joaquin Valley ran dry. Additionally, about 40 other water districts in and around the San Joaquin Valley still have not installed residential OR commercial meters

In May of 2013, specifics of a so-called Delta water plan, put together over the preceding 7 years, were revealed. Basically, the plan calls for two enormous tunnels to be built that would redirect Sacramento River water under the San Joaquin Delta and send it to southern California communities. The price tag to build and operate these tunnels is estimated at $25 billion. Irrigation districts and retail water agencies would be responsible for funding two-thirds of the cost with the remainder coming from state and federal coffers.

Whether federal fisheries will sign off on this project is anyone's guess but the entities involved have agreed to restore huge swaths of habitat in an effort to avert endangered native species regulations.

The Metropolitan Water District of Southern California has projected that this scheme would add up to $84 to the average household's annual water bill but opponents predict the additional sum will be much greater.

In 2014, the state finally passed a multi-billion dollar water bond designed to address more underground storage and conveyance as well as increased pressure and education on water conservation. Actually, refitting elder agricultural irrigation to state-of-the-art systems with public money would solve most of California's water supply woes for the ensuing two or three decades and would cost much less than building tunnels or subterranean storehouses but using government funds to benefit private concerns is always touchy subject at best, even when practical and economical.

ALTERNATIVE SOURCES ARE COSTLY

Item: According to its 2010 Urban Water Management Plan, the South Coast Water District (SCWD) imports 80 percent of its drinking water from Northern California and the Colorado River. This is not unusual. Many water agencies in the state do not have enough precipitation or above ground water sources (like lakes or rivers) to supply current, much less growing, populations.

Back in 2009, SCWD's water deliveries were cut dramatically due to drought and a series of judicial rulings protecting certain imperiled flora and fauna species like the Delta Smelt. SCWD directors have been evaluating and pursuing alternative water sources, including a desalination (salt removal) plant near Laguna Beach designed to refine brackish (high mineral content) water taken from underneath the ocean, a project led by the Municipal Water District of Orange County. The initial construction costs, estimated up to $150 million, would be spread among program participants that might include San Clemente, San Juan Capistrano, Laguna Beach County Water District, Moulton Niguel Water District and South Coast Water District.

Many regular folks like you and I think of desalination as the perfect solution to the world's water crisis but it isn't nearly the be-all, end-all amateur hydrologists have been led to expect. First and foremost, taking mineral content out of water consumes inordinate amounts of energy.

In just one example, the late renowned hydro-geologist Dr. Pierre Saint-Amand, whose early work in geology was his theory of the rotation of the Pacific Ocean Basin, often stated, when discussing desal, that it would require more energy to take the salt out of one gallon of ocean water than it would to pump a gallon of fresh water from Northern California over a mountain range to Southern California.

Recently, the Wessex Institute estimated an average cost of producing an acre foot of potable water in California between $300 and $600. In the same study, and in other feasibility investigations including one by the Indian Wells Valley Water District, converting high saline/mineral water to drinkable liquid could cost as much as $2,000 per acre foot.

Yes, the price of water is definitely going UP.

The San Diego County Water Authority is seeking to buy all the processed sea water produced by a Carlsbad desalination plant expected to produce 50 million gallons of drinkable water a day. The deal – which would make the desalination factory, the largest in the Western Hemisphere, is awaiting approval by the water authority board.

The project comes at the steep cost of around $900 million. Supplies would be used for about 7 percent of the San Diego region and would be funded by bonds. It could cost San Diego up to $2,300 for an acre-foot of water. (See AP story as printed in the _New York Times_)

Of course, price isn't the only problem. Opponents of desalination fear the process could change the pH of the affected oceanic eco system.

"Returning of brine into the sea, without dilution, may cause a rise in local salinity. This may lead to a change in the biological functioning of the local ecosystem. Ideally, one looks for a disposal point where the brine is diluted sufficiently to minimize the change in salinity. One should carefully consider the plant location, taking into account the point of intake as well as the position of discharge." [1]

RECENT

---

[1] Practical Experience in Designing and Operating Sea Water Reverse Osmosis Desalination Plants on the Island of Seychelles by Alan Joseph Sarkis

WATER REGULATIONS

Item: When federal arsenic standards were lowered in 2006 by the Environmental Protection Agency (EPA) from 50 parts per billion (ppb) to 10 ppb, thousands of America's water providers were alerted that they would soon be officially "out of compliance," and would be required to mitigate arsenic content through treatment. Because of this mandate, those agencies are now building or have finished building arsenic removal plants – an expensive enterprise. For example, the Indian Wells Valley Water District's (IWVWD) capital improvement investment for arsenic removal proved to be almost $13 million while the cost of running the two plants has been exceeding $650,000 annually. As the IWVWD serves slightly less than 30,000 customers through around 11,000 hookups, it's easy to imagine the sticker shock this construction produced at the agency's rates and fees which have been revised upward twice in four years and received another small boost in 2013.

USING MORE THAN WE HAVE

Item: According to measurements recorded by the U.S. Department of the Interior Bureau of Reclamation, the water level in Lake Mead officially dropped to 1,088 feet above sea level as of January 1, 2015, a number that has hovered for several years near the lowest elevation of the lake since the 1930s, when it was filling. (Please refer to the chart at http://www.usbr.gov/lc/region/g4000/hourly/mead-elv.html)

If the water level falls to 1,075 feet, the federal government will institute preset "low reservoir storage conditions," forcing the seven states that depend on the Colorado (Colorado, New Mexico, Utah, Arizona, California, and Nevada), as well as Mexico, to drastically cut water consumption pursuant to an agreement they all signed in 2007.

Unfortunately, extended drought has been compounded by the fact that the Colorado allotments were determined in the early 1920s, when, according to tree-ring data and sedimentation studies, the Colorado basin was substantially wetter than normal. If drought persists and more water is diverted from the Colorado River, Lake Mead could drop to 1,050 feet. That would prevent water from reaching the original intake pipe resulting in a 40 percent cut of Las Vegas' water supply. Additionally, Hoover Dam, constructed in 1935 to form Lake Mead, would be unable to fulfill its contract to provide electricity for 750,000 people in Los Angeles. To ensure stability on both the H2O and energy horizons, SNWA designed two more intake pipes, one of which has been completed. The third and last "straw" has hit several snags, and will not be up and running until late 2013 at the earliest – with an estimated cost of $700 million.

With an eye to planning for continued drought in the region, representatives of the seven states mentioned above met with the Department of the Interior and the Bureau of Reclamation in in May, 2013. The idea was to research and develop conservation recommendations agreed to by all the participants that would include reusing water, desalination, subterranean water banks and the transfer of water to urban areas from agriculture.

In connected business, Las Vegas and Henderson, Nevada have been acquiring neighboring water rights for decades. Now, all the water that can be allocated from the Colorado and other regional water sources has been allocated. Therefore, these two thirsty cities are now casting interested attention on groundwater supplies in a wildlife refuge in bordering Utah, a fact that has both ranchers and environmentalists outspokenly critical. The Southern Nevada Water Authority's (SNWA) situation has grown so problematic that officials have been planning on building a $3 billion pipeline to access 16 billion gallons of water per year from an aquifer in the Snake Valley on the Nevada/Utah boundary, a move referred to in the Nevada Press as "the greatest urban water grab in 100 years." But not so fast: in December, 2103, a judge has rebuffed state approval for this project in what is surely only the first in what will prove a long and expensive judicial tug of war.

Historical Note: In the early 1900s, William Mulholland sent Los Angeles Department of Water and Power agents, who were pretending to be representatives of the Bureau of Reclamation, to the Owens Valley in Inyo County, California. Their purpose was to surreptitiously buy property, thereby securing ownership of water from Owens Lake, the area aquifer and the Owens River. The clandestine mission was a complete success. Los Angeles became a center of finance, activity, population, etc. while Inyo County is … known for fishing, canoeing, hiking and other tourist activities.

Reference: (For both perspectives on this story, please see http://wsoweb.ladwp.com/Aqueduct/historyoflaa/ and *"The Owens Valley and the Los Angeles water controversy; Owens Valley as I knew it,"* by R. Coke Wood and *"Western Times and Water Wars: State, Culture, and Rebellion in California"* by John Walton.)

WATER CONSERVATION AND EDUCATION

Item: Over a 14 year period, Albuquerque residents saved well over a billion gallons of water – enough to provide for the entire city for three years – through restrictive landscape regulations, water recycling and reclamation and other measures. Interestingly, since 1990, Albuquerque's population has increased by 150.55 percent - as opposed to a 33.41 percent increase in New Mexico's population, according to Clrsearch.com Demographics.

Scary Bit of Information: When it comes to drought, the ancient record may have some bad news for North America: A number of "paleoclimatology" (ancient climate) studies have been conducted by scientists associated with NOAA involving such oddities as the Bristlecone Pine's tree rings (dendrochronology) and river and lake bed sedimentation samples.
(Please take a closer look at a fascinating examination of drought in North America from ancient times to the present: "North American Drought: A Paleo Perspective" http://www.ncdc.noaa.gov/paleo/drought/drght_home.html)

Item: The Indian Wells Valley Water District in California's high desert cajoled, persuaded and coaxed a 17% drop in per capita usage between 2007 and 2012. They certainly needed a water use makeover because: 1) their lone aquifer had been overpumped by over 1.3 million acre feet since the 1960s and no science in the world was or is sophisticated enough to accurately forecast how much pristine water was left. 2) the present day overdraft was amounting to 30,000 acre feet used annually minus only 9,000 acre feet in recharge. 3)

For the California and Arizona high desert regions, a history of weather patterns over the past 9,000 years has been researched by UCLA in conjunction with the University of Arizona. The findings demonstrate that, for most of that time span, 30 to 60 year droughts were not unusual and 100-plus year droughts were not uncommon.

Just consider, for a moment, what a 120 year drought would look like in your neighborhood.

In rural Kern County, the pre-program consumer thought process amounted to something like "It's my water and I'll do exactly what I want to with it." A tunnel-visioned attitude toward this precious communal asset is understandable as water works are invisible – buried under ground or constructed on the outskirts of town – and most people rarely think about or understand the realities of water production.

A winningly innovative combination of educational tools changed minds and hearts. It began with a continuous flow of breezy, accessibly written press releases about water systems in general, the District's particular water situation, system maintenance requirements, well replacement costs, mainline replacement routines, water treatment technology, District staff profiles, etc. There were all manner of children's programs, like conservation-themed calendar contests and a specially composed song called: *I Love Water; Water Loves Me.*

The Board passed Landscape ordinances utilizing both sticks and carrots regulating grass for new Construction and limiting watering days and hours for 6 months each year. There were dry climate gardening showcases; hilarious ads; a conservation-themed song sung by the Board and played on radio called *Save All the Water You Can* to the music of *Winter Wonderland.*

The District provided funding for Xeriscape gardens at schools; an award-winning Ambassador Program that gave free Xeriscape landscape sketches and other assistance for those who wished to convert grass ... you name it, they tried it ... innovation after innovation ... and it all worked.

Conservation is a fantastic tool in the sustainability arsenal because conserved water is the cheapest water there is. Why? Because the wells are already drilled; the pipes have already been installed; and the make-up of the water is a known commodity. So, a greater reliance on conservation strategies and water reuse in all its many forms seems like a great place to start.

Media coverage chronicles the fact that cities across the West and Southwest have been implementing increasingly strict water efficiency, re-use and conservation requirements even as drought conditions across the country spread and lengthen. But what if these dry climate tales are the tip of an iceberg? Each year, the American Society of Civil Engineers grades the nation's crumbling infrastructure: levees, dams, wells, storage tanks, etc. Water works have habitually received a D- with the Society estimating that 7 billion gallons of water a day are lost due to leaks. (**http://www.infrastructurereportcard.org/fact-sheet/drinking-water**)

In a similarly discomfiting vein, the American Water Works Association and other expert entities on the subject predict that, over the next 20 to 30 years, more than half of America's potable water infrastructure will have to be replaced, including cast-iron pipes installed in the late 19th century. Those pipes' 120-year life span is approaching the end of a shelf life. And let's not forget the pipes installed in the 1920s that were only supposed to last for a century or the pipes laid following World War II that are expected to last for about 75 years.

According to the EPA's Aging Water Infrastructure Research Program, there are already an estimated 240,000 water main breaks each year in the United States and the cost to fix these problems are estimated at over $300 billion.

These are just a few examples of "water situations" that all point to one conclusion: the price of water is going UP!

IS WATER THE NEXT OIL?

Within the past few years, media stories have begun referring to water as "the next commodity" and prophesied that water would soon be traded on the open market like diamonds, oil or gold.

Both Ted Turner and T. Boone Pickens have huge water holdings. In fact, Pickens now heads Mesa Water Inc., which controls water rights covering over 100,000 acres of the Ogallala aquifer. Right now foreign and domestic for-profit companies are buying up and privatizing small

American water agencies. Can private interests here or abroad balance a profitable bottom line while providing safe, clean and, most importantly, affordable water for now and the generations to come? All other commodities have substitutes but no living thing on this planet can exist without "blue gold."

CONCLUSIONS

Most hydrologists, water managers, environmentalists and other experts in this field will tell you that conserved water is the cheapest water there is – or will ever be. Why? Because the wells are already drilled; the pipes have already been installed and the make-up of the water is a known commodity with appropriate treatment plants in place. So a greater reliance on conservation practices and water reuse in all its many forms seem like common sense solutions.

Replacing thirsty residential landscaping like lawns with drought friendly grasses, plants and shrubs and holding large water users to account through metering and appropriately tiered rates are steps that can be taken today.

Here's a thought: Maybe it's time to replace what NASA calls the number one irrigated "crop" in the U.S. – grass (40 million acres worth) – with something more sustainable that doesn't cost $40 billion a year to mow, feed, edge, weed and haul away.

Is it time to rethink what the phrase "a beautiful garden" means to a more water aware culture?

Seeking additional sources of water is always an important tool of prudent water management. Of course, procuring sources from outside a jurisdiction will entail movement and treatment – and leave the newly exploited area in danger of subsidence over the long haul.

There are solutions that can be used in combination:

- Water agencies need to expand education and outreach efforts, while actively supporting all manner of innovative and interactive educational opportunities. These might include pushing free indoor and outdoor conservation gadgets, providing DIY dry climate garden workshops, creating colorful and catchy written materials and other handouts to spice up all community education and outreach efforts for schools, businesses and other civic entities.

- When done correctly, free water audits for homes and businesses can pinpoint wasteful water habits, malfunctioning irrigation, leaks, non-efficient toilets and showerheads that should be replaced, etc. Audits help save water and lower water bills – and are also a great way to build respect and trust with customers.

- Proper watering techniques using the most cutting edge technology – ranging from rotary sprinkler heads to satellite-run irrigation "smart timers" – are a must. In fact, the greatest potential water savings would be the conversion of all appropriate agriculture to 21st Century drip tape, bubbler or subterranean irrigation that concentrates on delivering moisture to plant roots, lessening evaporation. And, since converting from flood irrigation to more efficient methods can be too expensive for small operations, using public money to help accomplish the changeover would prove smart over time. World water and climate expert Dr. Peter Gleick of the Pacific Institute has said that modernizing California's agricultural watering practices would go a long way in solving California's water problems because agriculture accounts for 80 percent of all usage.

- Effective and prudent long-term resource stewardship takes community awareness, involvement, intercession and commitment. A Board of Directors or a management team will be responsive to constituent needs only when voters vote and questions and concerns are raised and answered at public meetings, hopefully covered by an interested and informed press.

- Water consumers need to take a more active role. For instance, do you know where your water comes from? What shape is your water delivery system in? Do you know which minerals or contaminants are present in your water and in what percentages? Does your water agency chlorinate? How much does it cost your utility company to produce an acre foot of water? Knowing the answer to these questions can help you decide whether your water agency is doing its job or not – and it may alter your attitude toward your own water-wise practices.

CLOSING THOUGHTS:

Water is indispensable to life; no living thing can exist, much less thrive, without it. Our children and grandchildren deserve a future where they can enjoy the benefits of a safe and affordable water supply – benefits that go far beyond our everyday survival and influence our joyful experience of Planet Earth. Working together, we can reshape the future of H2O in America. What better time to start than today?

CHARTS and GRAPHICS

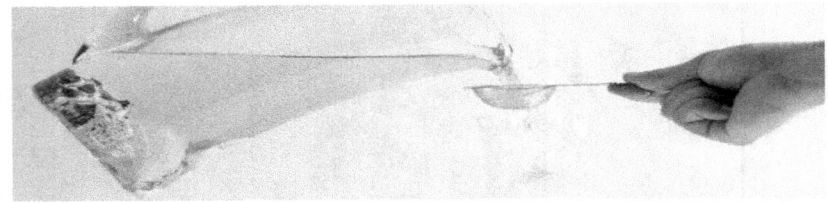

The proposed 30-year Water Purchase Agreement between Poseidon Resources and the San Diego County Water Authority to purchase desalinated seawater from the Carlsbad Desalination Plant was recently released to the public.

Desalination process flow chart

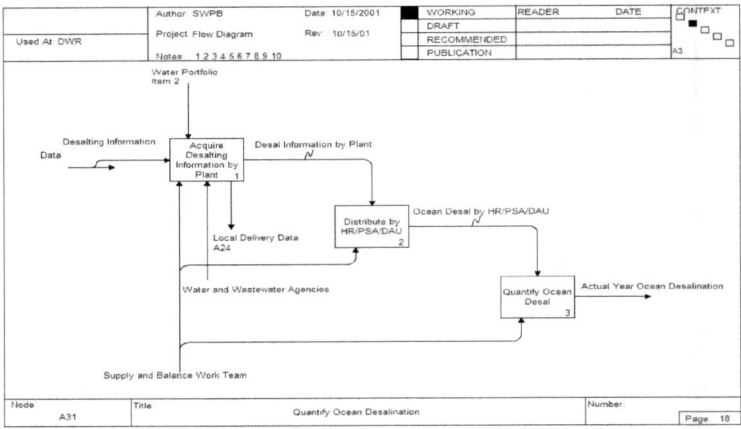

Photos are Public Domain as posted by the sites listed

Infrastructure Report Card by American Society of Civil Engineers
(http://www.infrastructurereportcard.org/fact-sheet/drinking-water)

ESTIMATED 5-YEAR FUNDING
REQUIREMENTS FOR
**DRINKING WATER AND
WASTEWATER**

Total investment needs
$255 BILLION

Estimated spending
$146.4 BILLION
Projected shortfall
$108.6 BILLION

EPA's Infrastructure Report:

As posted on their website http://www.epa.gov/awi/distributionsys.html

- There are 240,000 water main breaks per year in the United States.
- A 2005 British study correlated self-reported diarrhea with low water-pressure events (including water main breaks).
- The number of breaks increases substantially near the end of the system's service life. Large utility breaks in the Midwest increased from 250 per year to 2,200 per year during a 19-year period. In 2003, Baltimore, Maryland, reported 1,190 water main breaks—that's more than three per day.

EPA has estimated that if spending for capital investment and operations and maintenance remain at current levels, the potential gap in funding for 2000–2019 would be approximately $263 billion for our drinking water infrastructure.

Public Domain Photo from EPA Site / Infrastructure Graphic from American Society of Civil Engineers

REFERENCES:

US Drought Map: The U.S. Drought Monitor is produced in partnership between the National Drought Mitigation Center at the University of Nebraska-Lincoln, the United States Department of Agriculture, and the National Oceanic and Atmospheric Administration. (http://droughtmonitor.unl.edu/)

Perils Of Over Pumping:

- San Joaquin Valley Mining underground Report
http://pubs.usgs.gov/circ/circ1182/pdf/06SanJoaquinValley.pdf

- Study on Coachella Valley Sinking
http://ca.water.usgs.gov/projects/coachella.html

- Department of Water Resources, Bulletin 108, Coachella Valley Investigation, 1964 and Coachella Valley Water District

Alternative Resources Are Costly:

- The South Coast Water District is seeking to include ocean desalination in South County and has formed a Project Participant Committee with members from the cities of San Clemente and San Juan Capistrano, Laguna Beach County Water District, Moulton Niguel Water District and South Coast Water District. The Municipal Water District is a Project Supporter.
http://www.scwd.org/water/watersupply/desalplant.asp

- A 2004 Great Lakes Commission Report on Applications of Water Conservation and Technology Practices around the World
http://www.glc.org/wateruse/conservation/pdf/BestTechnologiesReport.pdf

- Wessex Institute Study
http://library.witpress.com/pages/PaperInfo.asp?PaperID=17561

- Fresno Water Meter Paper:
http://fresnowatermeter.org/

- Sacramento Water Utility Meter Plan:
http://www.cityofsacramento.org/utilities/water/water-meters.cfm

Using More Than We Have:

- Colorado River Agreement
http://www.ose.state.nm.us/PDF/News/2007/pr-2007-05-01-7StatesAgreement.pdf

- Hoover Dam
North American Drought: A Paleo Perspective:
http://www.ncdc.noaa.gov/paleo/drought/drght_home.html
Southern Nevada Water Authority and the Hoover Dam Web Site:
http://www.usbr.gov/lc/hooverdam/educate/index.html

Water Conservation And Education:

- (Please take a closer look at a fascinating examination of drought in North America from ancient times to the present: "North American Drought: A Paleo Perspective" http://www.ncdc.noaa.gov/paleo/drought/drght_home.html)

- Costs of Infrastructure:

The Water Infrastructure Network
http://win-water.org/legislativecenter/toby3_27_0.shtml

General Accounting Office, Water Infrastructure: Comprehensive Asset Management Has Potential to Help Utilities Better Identify Needs and Plan Future Investments
http://www.gao.gov/new.items/d04461.pdf

Environmental Protection Agency, Clean Water and Drinking Water Infrastructure GAP Analysis Report; and American Water Works Association, Dawn of the Replacement Era: Reinvesting in Drinking Water Infrastructure http://www.win-water.org/reports/infrastructure.pdf

Aging Water Infrastructure
http://www.epa.gov/awi/basic.html

- Infrastructure Report Card by American Society of Civil Engineers
(**http://www.infrastructurereportcard.org/fact-sheet/drinking-water**)

Is Water The Next Oil?

- http://finance.yahoo.com/news/water-next-big-commodity-174655313.html

- http://www.thedailycrux.com/Post/30889/World-s-best-investor-goes-long-water

Other Material:

- Water.Org
http://water.org/water-crisis/water-facts/water/

- National Oceanic and Atmospheric Administration

- http://www.serconline.org/waterPrivatization/fact.html

- http://www.epa.gov/WaterSense/pubs/supply.html

- http://earthobservatory.nasa.gov/Features/Lawn/lawn2.php

- http://www.backyardnature.com/cgi-bin/gt/tpl.h,content=381

- http://worldwater.org/chronology.html

ABOUT the AUTHOR

Lucinda Sue Crosby is an award winning journalist and environmentalist who spent five years as coordinator of education and conservation for a retail California water agency. The opinions expressed in this essay are the author's and not necessarily those of the sources sited, nor did the author receive compensation or remuneration from any of the sources consulted for the publication of this article.

Crosby is also an award-winning author, named in 2011 by The Authors Show as "One of 50 Great Authors You Should be Reading," and she is a Kindle International Bestseller of three books:

Francesca of Lost Nation – Four-time Literary Prize winner for Romance/Adventure Fiction
http://amzn.to/Qu7FkB

The Cancer Club: a crazy, sexy, inspirational novel of survival - Top-ten finalist in the Next Best Fiction Author Contest by Hampton Roads Publishing and Hierophant Publishing
Significant inspiration for this book was provided by the writings and life of stage and TV actress and Jim Henson puppeteer Eren Ozker (1948 -1993)
http://amzn.to/1DctAXf

The Adventures of Baylard Bear – a story about being DIFFERENT – International Book Finalist for Children's Fiction with Adoption Theme
http://amzn.to/OvKU2O

Why is POOKIE stinky? For Ages 4 to 7 Years Old (Book One: "Silly" Puppy Series 1 – A terrier story about an adopted dog written in verse suitable for beginning readers and written for children 5 to 8 years-old
http://amzn.to/1u5X07v

$ell more Ebook$ - How to increase sales and Amazon rankings using Kindle Direct Publishing
http://amzn.to/V9LEMI

Advanced Kindle Book Marketing: How to Sell more Ebooks online with new Amazon promotions and Kindle Bestseller Tips - Advanced Kindle Book Marketing Tools - 2014 and 2015 promo tips
http://amzn.to/1zR3JVh

Thank you for your time and purchase. You can reach me at: luckycinda@yahoo.com.

www.ingramcontent.com/pod-product-compliance
Lightning Source LLC
Chambersburg PA
CBHW071352310526
45790CB00018B/1427